Animals Attack!

Constrictors

Maurice Gray

KIDHAVEN PRESS
An imprint of Thomson Gale, a part of The Thomson Corporation

THOMSON
GALE™

Detroit • New York • San Francisco • San Diego • New Haven, Conn. • Waterville, Maine • London • Munich

THOMSON
GALE

For more information, contact
KidHaven Press
27500 Drake Rd.
Farmington Hills, MI 48331-3535
Or you can visit our Internet site at http://www.gale.com

LIBRARY OF CONGRESS CATALOGING-IN-PUBLICATION DATA

Gray, Maurice.
Constrictors / by Maurice Gray.
p. cm. — (Animals attack)
Includes bibliographical references.
ISBN 0-7377-3005-6 (hard cover : alk. paper)
1. Pythons—Juvenile literature. 2. Anaconda—Juvenile literature. 3. Snake attacks—Juvenile literature. I. Title. II. Series.
QL666.O63G73 2005
597.96'7—dc22

2005009014

Printed in the United States of America

Contents

Chapter 1

Giant Snakes

Fourteen-year-old Petrus Mthembu was a goatherd in Natal, South Africa, in 1982 when a huge python attacked him. He not only survived the attack, but he later told his story, first to his local newspaper, and then to the *National Enquirer.* Although the newspapers reported some details differently, both stories tell how Petrus was forced to kill the snake to survive.

Petrus was on his way to round up some of his goats near his home when the python burst out from a clump of bushes and attacked him. It threw its body across Petrus and wrapped him in its coils before Petrus could move. "I sent up a desperate prayer," Petrus said. "Please God, don't let me finish my life as a snake's breakfast!"[1]

Petrus had a small knobbed stick that he used to herd the goats. When the python opened its mouth to bite him, he jammed the stick into its mouth. It locked onto the knob on top of the stick with its mouth and tightened its coils around Petrus at the same time. He tried to pull the stick out of the python's mouth, but when he did, the stick fell out of his hand and landed on the ground out of his reach.

With no other weapons at hand, Petrus bit the snake's throat and tore out some of its flesh. The snake jerked away from this unexpected attack, and then tried to bite Petrus again. Petrus beat him

The coils of this enormous reticulated python are strong enough to strangle a human being.

to it, and bit the python again, harder than he did the first time. His teeth struck bone this time, and the python relaxed its grip and died soon after.

Petrus was able to wiggle free, but he was shaken by the experience. "My whole body was badly bruised," Petrus said, "and my two front teeth were chipped. I staggered home with the snake draped around my neck. My family and I skinned the python and ate the meat. I still have the snake skin–I plan to keep it, to remind me of God's goodness in sparing my life."[2]

What Are Constrictors?

Constrictors are snakes that use their bodies to kill their victims. They bite their prey first, and once they have a grip, they coil their bodies around the victim and force the air from its body. When the victim breathes out, the constrictor tightens its grip so that it cannot breathe in again. The victim suffocates quickly.

Anacondas and certain species of pythons (including Indian pythons, **reticulated** pythons, and African rock pythons) are the only constrictors in the world that grow large enough to threaten human beings. These snakes are also known as giant snakes. **Herpetologists** (reptile scientists) use the term *giant snake* to describe snakes that grow to be at least 20 feet (6.1m) long. Anacondas are native to South America, and pythons are found across Africa, India, and Central Asia.

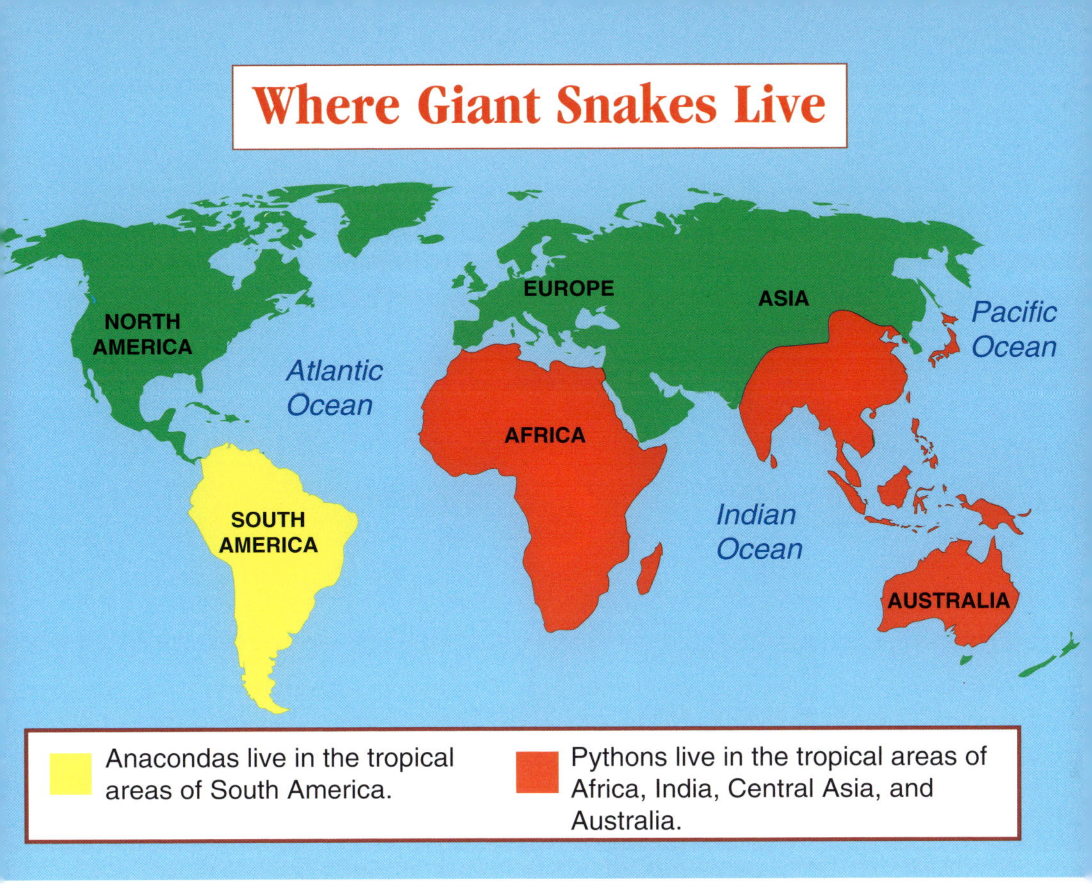

Constrictor Advantages

Constrictors are built for surprise attacks against victims who are alone. Because constrictors are large and slow, they hunt by ambushing their **prey**. Constrictors are green, yellow, brown, gray, dark red, or some combination of all of those colors. Their coloring allows them to hide under piles of leaves, in bushes, or under the surface of a lake or stream. This natural camouflage is combined with these giant snakes' abilities to hold perfectly still for hours on end. This allows them nearly perfect invisibility to people and animals in their area until it is too late. Although constrictors usually move slowly, they can

Built to Attack

strike far faster than a person can recognize the danger and move out of the way. A constrictor's strength is far greater than that of a person. So, once a constrictor traps a person in its coils, it is nearly impossible for that person to break free without help. When a constrictor attacks a victim from the water, it often drags its prey into the water, where it drowns.

Like all snakes, constrictors have the added advantage of fear. Human beings naturally tend to fear snakes. Whether it is because of their size, the reputation giant snakes have gained (through movies such as the 1997 *Anaconda* and its 2004 sequel), or simply lack of knowledge, many people are deeply afraid of snakes. Herpetologist Clifford Pope writes, "I must conclude that their secret weapon is an ability to paralyze the foe with terror."[3] His belief is that giant snakes use the fact that many animals are afraid of them to their advantage.

Surprise Attacks

Researchers E. Muthusamy and H. Gopalakrishnakone of India reported a surprise attack on a local man in 1990. The man was riding his bicycle near a creek at night when he dropped his flashlight. When he got off the bike to pick it up, a python exploded out of the creek and struck, biting his hand. The man managed to get clear before the python could coil around him. He escaped with cuts to his hand and no other injuries.

With its mouth open, a reticulated python prepares to strike with lightning speed.

One of the earliest recorded giant snake attacks happened in Brazil in 1863. Herpetologist H.W. Bates was studying anacondas in South America when he reported an attack on a neighbor's ten-year-old son. The father took his son with him to pick fruit, and while he worked, the boy amused himself in the nearby river. Bates reported that, without warning, an anaconda "stealthily wound its coils around him, unperceived until it was too late to escape."[4] The father heard his son's cries for help and rushed to his son's rescue. After a struggle, the father was forced to kill the anaconda to make it relax its grip. Bates reported that the man tore the snake's jaws open with his bare hands.

In this instance, the anaconda apparently concealed itself just below the surface of the river and waited until the boy came close enough for it to attack.

Risk of Attack

Fortunately for people who live in areas populated by constrictors, these giant snakes normally do not

A python in Kenya wraps its strong coils around the neck of a young waterbuck.

view human beings as prey. They prefer smaller prey such as wild pigs, small deer, birds, fish, and even other snakes. An average-sized adult human being is too big for a giant snake to safely attack, and the round head and shoulders of a human are difficult for a giant snake to easily swallow. However, if prey is scarce and people live nearby (as in the story above), a constrictor will go against the natural urge to avoid human contact and attack a child, or even a small adult. For that reason, people who live in areas populated by anacondas and pythons warn their children to be careful when they venture out into the forest or close to bodies of water. The best natural defense against a constrictor attack is to stay alert.

Chapter 2

Under Attack: When Humans Become Prey

As with all snakes, giant snakes recognize human beings as dangerous and avoid human contact whenever possible. When constrictors do attack human beings, they do it for one of three reasons: out of hunger, in self-defense, or by mistake.

Lina Attacks

Depending on the size of their last meal, giant snakes can go weeks or even months without eating. But if they get very hungry and cannot find anything else to eat, they will attack people for food.

Field biologist Maria Muñoz and two colleagues were involved in an ecological study of anacondas

In 2001 Lucas Sibanda of Pretoria, South Africa, had a close encounter with an African rock python that he will never forget. He was walking to work when the python attacked him from the brush. Sibanda froze with fear, and the python coiled around him. Because Sibanda had no weapons with him, he survived only by biting the python's throat. When the snake released him, he picked up a stick and beat it to death. Like his countryman Petrus Mthembu nearly twenty years earlier, Sibanda survived, but the encounter left him shaken.

Self-Defense

A constrictor defends itself first and foremost by hiding. If discovered, a constrictor reacts by swelling its body and hissing to warn its enemy off. If that does not work, the constrictor strikes and bites the intruder until it leaves. Constriction is not used as a defense weapon, but only as a way to kill food. Given that fact, the python that attacked Lucas Sibanda clearly did not see him as a threat, but as a potential meal.

Once a constrictor finds a favorite hunting place, it will defend that place against all intruders. Since their coloring makes them almost invisible to anyone or anything passing by, people can easily step on or near a hidden constrictor. Constrictors are threatened by this sort of accidental contact and will attack a person who comes too close to where they are hiding.

A biologist holds an anaconda by the neck to keep the snake from striking.

People kill snakes for their skin and meat, to protect their pets and livestock from attacks, or out of fear and disgust. Because of this, snakes recognize people as natural enemies along with wild pigs, birds, and other snakes. If a constrictor feels threatened, it may attack a person to keep that person

An anaconda in search of prey slithers through the vegetation of a marsh in Brazil.

from attacking it first. Although Muñoz and her fellow researchers decided that Lina's attack on her was due to hunger, the attack could also have been caused by the scientist invading the snake's territory.

By Mistake

Like most snakes, anacondas and pythons do not rely on eyesight as much as they rely on other senses. Snakes are not blind, but they do not see the way human beings see. Many snakes have difficulty seeing objects that are standing still, and they can detect movement only at close range. Their eyes see

Like most snakes, this anaconda has very poor eyesight and must rely on its other senses to hunt.

best at night. Because of this, many snakes are **nocturnal**.

All snakes have a strong sense of smell. They have an organ in the roof of the mouth called the **Jacobson's organ**, which acts for them like a nose. Their tongues sample odors and transmit them to the Jacobson's organ, which processes the different smells and allows the snake to tell one animal from another.

Giant snakes use a combination of different senses to hunt for food, including vision, vibration, smell, and heat. All of these senses have roles, but the most important is smell. The smell of food stimulates a snake to use its other senses in order to attack and eat.

Natural **predators**, constrictors use their sense of smell and ability to feel vibrations in the ground to tell when prey is coming. By the time something or someone gets close enough for a constrictor to attack, it has already smelled and felt its potential prey coming and decided whether to attack. Once the snake decides it is safe, it waits until it sees movement at a close enough range to attack.

In 1978 herpetologist William W. Lamar and two companions were on a study expedition in Colombia. One day when they were wading through a forest stream in knee-deep water to find giant snakes, a giant snake found them instead.

Still coiled around an antelope, a rocky python begins to swallow its prey whole.

“All of a sudden,” Lamar said, “an anaconda exploded out of the water.”[5] Without warning, the anaconda attacked the man to Lamar’s left and ripped his shirt off. As the giant snake gathered itself to make a second strike, Lamar quickly wheeled around and shot it to death.

At the time of the attack (mid-afternoon), the three men were following a game trail. Lamar decided for this reason that the attack was a case of hunger and mistaken identity. This anaconda, which they measured at nearly 25 feet (7.62m) long, was used to hunting in that area and was lying in ambush for prey. When Lamar and his companions entered the area, the anaconda may have mistaken Lamar and his companions for **peccaries**, **tapirs**, or other native animals that it usually eats, and attacked them.

Constrictor attacks on humans are rare. Giant snakes will avoid all contact with human beings when they can. If they are unexpectedly forced into contact with human beings, however, they will feel threatened, and when they feel threatened, they will defend themselves.

Chapter 3

When Captive Snakes Attack

In the 1930s, famous explorer Frank Buck had an experience with a python that reminded him just how dangerous capturing a snake can be. A python that Buck and his team were trying to capture turned the tables on them. They were tracking it through the woods when one of Buck's men stepped over a log and right onto the snake they were looking for. The python immediately bit the man's pants and then wrapped itself around him. Buck and the other three assistants quickly moved to help the captured man, and they managed to free him and secure the snake.

Back then pythons were taken captive either for research or to sell to zoos. Now there is more and

Despite the ferocious nature of Burmese pythons, these snakes are popular pets in the United States.

more interest in the United States, in pet giant snakes. Snake owners who are not careful with their exotic pet face danger.

Cartoonist Gary Larson (the *Far Side*) once owned a Burmese python; which he had raised from a baby. He got rid of it not long after it reached adulthood because it attacked him. Larson said that until the attack he had never thought a lot about the fact that he was "living with a gigantic

predator with a very small brain."[6]

Due to the increasing interest in, and availability of, Burmese pythons in the United States, a growing number of people own them. Giant snakes are predators by nature, and no matter how tame a snake may seem, it still has the instincts of a hunter.

James Yaklich of Beloit, Wisconsin, learned two years ago that keeping a giant snake as a pet is not always a good idea. Yaklich was the owner of a large albino python, which he kept in a glass cage. One night the snake somehow managed to slither out of its cage and explore the house, eventually finding its way into the bed of Yaklich's five-year-old son.

The boy apparently moved in his sleep and startled the snake, which caused it to attack. Yaklich awakened to hear his son screaming for help. When Yaklich got to the bedroom, according to the police report, he found the python coiled around his son's arm.

Yaklich, who stands 6 feet 3 inches (1.91m) tall and weighs 265 pounds (120.2kg), barely managed to free his son from the python's grip. "I wrestled with the snake for a half-hour, forty-five minutes before I got him off,"[7] Yaklich said. His son was treated at a hospital for cuts and bruises and released the same night.

Predatory Instincts

Snake owners should never allow a large snake to roam freely, especially in a room where people spend a lot of time. If they do, the snake will react as if it were in the wild. It will claim that room as its hunting ground and view anything in that room as potential food. Snake owners with small children particularly need to keep this in mind.

Bill Broyles of Fruitland Park, Florida, learned about the predatory instincts of a pet giant snake the hard way. Broyles's eighteen-month-old son, Nickolas, was playing in the yard when Broyles suddenly heard his son scream for help. He ran to investigate, and was startled to find his pet python wrapped around Nickolas. The python bit Broyles several times, but he managed to pry Nickolas out of the snake's coils. The snake slithered away but was captured a few houses away by animal control workers.

Nickolas needed surgery to repair deep wounds to his scalp and eyelids, but he made a full recovery. Broyles said that he did not know how his python got loose or how it ended up on the patio where his son was playing. He immediately signed away ownership of that snake.

This young Cambodian boy risks serious injury and even death as he cuddles with his pet python.

Some captive snakes attack their owners by mistake. Many snake owners have triggered attacks by handling the animal they were about to feed to their snake before handling their pet. According to seasoned snake owner Ed Ricciuti, "Handling a large hungry snake immediately after handling potential snake food is a serious error."[8]

Authorities in New York reported two pet snake attacks in a five-year period. In 1996 a nineteen-year-old man was killed while trying to feed his python. The young man bought a live chicken to feed the python. He put the chicken down and went to get the snake, intending to take the snake out of its enclosure and carry it to the room where the chicken waited. However, when he opened the

This wildlife educator uses his captive albino Burmese python to teach children about large snakes.

cage, the snake smelled chicken on his hands. Thinking it was feeding time, the snake attacked the first thing within reach–its owner. The man was alone and could not unwrap the snake from his neck. Tragically, he died.

In 1999 a two-year-old girl in Buffalo, New York, managed to escape serious injury after her family's pet python tried to crush and swallow her. The snake got loose from its enclosure somehow and roamed around their house. It ate the girl's pet rabbit first. When it smelled the rabbit's scent on the girl, it considered her to be more food and attacked her next.

When her father found her, the snake had wrapped itself around the little girl's neck and bitten her forearm. He called for help. After the police helped him unwrap the snake from his daughter, they removed the snake from the house and killed it.

For safety reasons, snake owners should use extreme caution when handling their unique pets. When for any reason a constrictor attacks a person, it is almost impossible for the person to get free without help. People who keep giant snakes as pets should also take care to learn the potential dangers involved. Captive snake attacks can be avoided if owners handle their snakes properly.

Constrictor Safety Rules

Because smell is so important to a constrictor, it may mistake a person who has the smell of an animal on or near them for smaller prey. Constrictors in the wild have sometimes attacked people walking with dogs, goats, or chickens because the smell of those animals sets off their feeding instincts. Constrictors kept as pets are likely to do the same when they smell something on a person they like to eat. For this reason, great care should be taken to avoid confusing a pet snake during feeding time. Never approach a constrictor after handling a potential prey animal (live or dead), or when any potential prey animal is in the area.

The outline of a dog can be seen in the belly of this python caught on the streets of Manila in the Philippines.

People who handle constrictors must take the proper precautions to avoid attacks.

Ricciuti also explains that no matter how tame a pet snake is, its owner should never startle it. A snake's nature is to attack when startled. Nothing a pet owner tries to tame this instinct in their pet snake will work. If a constrictor is startled, it will constrict. If it becomes startled while hanging around someone's neck, the potential for disaster is great.

Chapter 4

Preventing a Constrictor Attack

Giant snakes do not need to eat often enough to pose a major threat to human life. While mammals need to eat often, giant snakes can go for weeks and even months without eating if prey is not available. After a large meal, a python or an anaconda is not likely to attack anything, especially a person, until it becomes hungry again. Naturally, a giant snake that has not eaten in a very long time is more likely to attack a human being.

Safety Precautions

Although giant snakes do not attack human beings often, people who live near them in the wild learn how to prevent attacks. Because such attacks are rare,

Having just swallowed a capybara, this anaconda will not have to eat again for weeks.

there is no single, set strategy. People in areas where giant snakes live know that they should stay alert when they are in heavy brush or around bodies of water. They know that these places are where giant snakes like to lie in ambush.

According to the *Kenya Times* in 1993, a python attacked a two-year-old child from a town near Mombasa. The boy was playing near his home

A South American man keeps a safe distance from a green anaconda.

when the python sneaked up and swallowed the child up to his waist. A man passing by saw what was happening and attacked the snake with a stone. The python spit the boy out unharmed, and the man beat the snake to death. In that instance, the man's awareness of the danger and quick response saved the boy's life.

In Africa and India in particular, people who keep domesticated animals learn to make sure that their animals' areas are secure against giant snake attacks. If a constrictor discovers that it can raid a chicken coop, it might also attack the owners of the chickens if they come around while the snake is there. Sealing all openings large enough for a python or anaconda to slip through keeps both livestock and owners safe.

A woman in Boston recently needed help from her son and the police to pry her pet Burmese python off of her arm and leg after it coiled around her while she was feeding it. The owner realized that her python was just being a python and convinced the police not to kill the snake afterward. She and her son both learned a lesson about owning and handling a large snake. She survived her encounter because she was not alone when the snake attacked. Also, both she and her son remained calm and called for help when they realized that they could not get the snake off her by themselves.

While giant snakes are native only to South America, Africa, India, and Central Asia, there is now a threat of giant snakes in the wild in the United States. Rangers who work in the Florida Everglades now have to be cautious due to an increasing population of Burmese pythons living there. This python population

A team of Australian zookeepers carries a Burmese python that was found slithering along the streets of Sydney.

is made up of former pet snakes that were discarded by owners. After deciding they did not want to keep their exotic pets, they simply released them into the wild. These natives of India have lived in the Everglades long enough to breed and now claim the Everglades as their natural habitat. Since the mid-1990s, rangers and other employees have captured and either removed or killed 67 Burmese pythons at Everglades National Park. There are no reported human fatalities caused by these snakes, but rangers and visitors to the park have to remain alert to the presence of these newcomers. The pythons sometimes stretch out across roads, which could cause traffic accidents. Park employees have reported incidents where tourists have gotten out of their cars to move what they thought was a large branch from the road, only to be alarmed when a huge snake slithered away as they approached.

Aside from the threat to park workers and visitors, the presence of these giant snakes in the Everglades threatens native animals. For example, they threaten indigo snakes by competing with them for food and territory, and wood storks by eating them. The federal government lists both the indigo snake and the wood stork as threatened species.

Tracking Pythons

Since the Burmese pythons are still newcomers to the Everglades, park officials are hopeful that they can still get all of them out even though they are breeding comfortably in their new environment.

Burmese python hatchlings in the Florida Everglades break out of their shells.

The plan is to find and remove all Burmese pythons from the Everglades while their numbers are still small enough to have a chance to do so.

In order to avoid attacks by these intruders and to eliminate the threat both to humans and to the native species of the Everglades, park officials recently came up with a way to track the giant snakes so that they can get rid of them. Lori Oberhofer, an Everglades wildlife technician, used trained dogs to track brown snakes while working for the U.S. Department of Agriculture in Guam. In her current position, she intends to use them to locate Burmese pythons.

Lori is currently training a beagle puppy, using either a python-scented rag or an actual Burmese python in a burlap bag for him to practice on. "Python Pete" is not allowed to run free in the park. During his training and beyond, he will be kept on a short leash to keep him from becoming prey for the giant snakes. If Python Pete trains well, Oberhofer will seek funding

Python Pete sniffs at a young python as he is trained to find populations of the constrictor living in the Everglades.

to train more dogs. Park biologists have a goal of preventing constrictors from attacking human beings by removing every last Burmese python from the Everglades. To do this, park visitors are encouraged to report giant snake sightings to any park official they see. When reports come in, Python Pete will be sent out to do his job. Once he finds the snake, park officials will either relocate it or put it to death in a humane way.

Constrictors, like other wild creatures, are dangerous and should be treated with caution. However, by being alert and informed, people can live free of worry of being attacked by giant snakes, either in the wild or by those kept as pets. Those who have been attacked and have lived to tell about it will never forget the experience.

Notes

Chapter 1: Giant Snakes

1. Quoted in John C. Murphy and Robert W. Henderson, *Tales of Giant Snakes: A Historical Natural History of Anacondas and Pythons.* Malabar, FL: Krieger, 1997, pp. 152–53.
2. Quoted in Murphy and Henderson, *Tales Of Giant Snakes,* p. 154.
3. Clifford H. Pope, *The Giant Snakes: The Natural History of the Boa Constrictor, the Anaconda and the Largest Pythons.* New York: Alfred A. Knopf, 1961 p. 225.
4. Quoted in Murphy and Henderson, *Tales Of Giant Snakes,* p. 133.

Chapter 2: Under Attack: When Humans Become Prey

5. Quoted in Murphy and Henderson, *Tales Of Giant Snakes,* p. 138.

Chapter 3: When Captive Snakes Attack

6. Quoted in Lee Krystek, "Big Snakes," Museum of Unnatural Mystery. www.unmuseum.org/bigsnake.htmg.

7. Quoted in JS Online, "Exotic Pets Under Scrutiny," www.jsonline.com/news/state/may01/python 19051801.asp?format=print.
8. Ed Ricciuti, *The Snake Almanac: A Fully Illustrated Natural History of Snakes Worldwide*. New York: Lyons Press, 2001, p. xiii.

Glossary

constrictors: Snakes that kill by coiling around their prey and suffocating it.

herpetologists: People who study snakes, lizards, and other reptiles.

Jacobson's organ: A small device in the roof of a snake's mouth that gives them their sense of smell.

nocturnal: Active at night.

peccaries: Wild pigs native to South America.

predators: Animals that kill other animals for food.

prey: Animals a constrictor hunts for food.

reticulated: Divided or marked with crossing lines or veins (like a net).

tapirs: South American mammals the size of a small horse.

For Further Exploration

Books

John C. Murphy and Robert W. Henderson, *Tales of Giant Snakes: A Historical Natural History of Anacondas and Pythons*. Malabar, FL: Krieger, 1997.

Clifford H. Pope, *The Giant Snakes: The Natural History of the Boa Constrictor, the Anaconda and the Largest Pythons*. New York: Alfred A. Knopf, 1961.

Ed Ricciuti, *The Snake Almanac: A Fully Illustrated Natural History of Snakes Worldwide*. New York: Lyons Press, 2001.

Peter Stafford, *Pythons and Boas*. Neptune, NJ: TFH, 1993.

Web Sites

Electronic Telegraph (www.telegraph.com). This is a daily news Web site that reports stories from across the country, and sometimes all over the world.

Melissa Kaplan's Herp and Green Iguana Information Collection (www.anapsid.org). This site helps people learn about the captive care requirements of many types of reptiles and amphibians. Includes a special section for kids.

The Museum of Unnatural Mystery (www.unmuseum.org). This site specializes in strange and interesting scientific facts, ranging in topic from UFOs to dinosaurs to reptiles.

National Geographic Kids (www.nationalgeographickids.com). This site provides information about a variety of topics.

Index

Picture Credits

Cover image: The Image Bank/Getty Images
AP/Wide World Photos, 28, 37, 40
Gary Braasch/The Image Bank/Getty Images, 14
Robert Caputo/Aurora Photos, 17
Erik De Castro/Reuters/Landov, 30
Francois Gohier/Photo Researchers, Inc., 34
Jan Lindblad/Photo Researchers, Inc., 35
Sven-Olof Lindblad/Photo Researchers, Inc., 11
© Joe McDonald/CORBIS, 10, 39
© Joe McDonald/Visuals Unlimited, 24
© Claus Meyer/Minden Pictures, 18
© Fritz Polking/Visuals Unlimited, 21
Powerphoto, 8 (image)
Reuters/Landov, 5
Suzanne Santillan, 7, 8
© Kevin Schafer/CORBIS, 19
Chor Sokunthea/Reuters/Landov, 27
© Kennan Ward/CORBIS, 31

About the Author

Maurice Gray is the author of one novel, *To Whom Much Is Given,* and "Traveling Mercies," a short story appearing in the national best-selling anthology, *Blessed Assurance.* He lives with his family in New Castle, Delaware, where he is currently at work on a new novel.